A Note to Parents and Teachers

Eyewitness Readers is a compelling new reading programme for children. *Eyewitness* has become the most trusted name in illustrated books, and this new series combines the highly visual *Eyewitness* approach with engaging, easy-to-read stories. Each *Eyewitness Reader* is guaranteed to capture a child's interest while developing his or her reading skills, general knowledge and love of reading.

The books are written by leading children's authors and are designed in conjunction with literacy experts, including Cliff Moon M.Ed., Honorary Fellow of the University of Reading. Cliff Moon spent many years as a teacher and teacher educator specializing in reading. He has written more than 140 books for children and teachers, and he reviews regularly for teachers' journals.

The four levels of *Eyewitness Readers* are aimed at different reading abilities, enabling you to choose the books that are exactly right for each child.

Level 1 – Beginning to read
Level 2 – Beginning to read alone
Level 3 – Reading alone
Level 4 – Proficient readers

The "normal" age at which a child begins to read can be anywhere from three to eight years old, so these levels are only guidelines.

No matter which level you select, you can be sure that you're helping children learn to read, then read to learn!

LEUCHARS PRIMARY SCHOOL

www.dk.com

Project Editors Penny Smith
and Caroline Bingham
Designer Andrew Burgess
Senior Editor Linda Esposito
Deputy Managing Art Editor
Jane Horne
Production Kate Oliver
Picture Researcher Jo Carlill
Illustrator Peter Dennis

Reading Consultant
Cliff Moon M.Ed.

Published in Great Britain by
Dorling Kindersley Limited
9 Henrietta Street
London WC2E 8PS

6 8 10 9 7 5

Visit us on the World Wide Web at http://www.dk.com

A CIP catalogue record for this book is
available from the British Library.

ISBN 0-7513-5736-7

Colour reproduction by Colourscan, Singapore
Printed and bound in Belgium by Proost

The publisher would like to thank the following for their
kind permission to reproduce their photographs:
t=top, b=below, l=left, r=right, c=centre,
BC=back cover, FC=front cover
Archive Photos: 3b, 4br, 18tr, 25, 47tr; **Corbis-Bettmann:**
9br, 22br, 30b; **Finley Holiday Film Corporation:** 7t;
Frank Spooner Pictures: 47br; **Hulton Getty:** 2cr, 26l,
36br; **Michael Freeman:** 17tr, 24br, 34br, 40br; **NASA:**
1br, 5, 7br, 8t, 15, 16b, 20tr, 21, 28br, 31, 32br, 37c, 44b,
46t, 46b; **Rex Features:** FC, 4tr, 27br, 29br, 32t, 33r, 45tr,
48br; **Robert Opie:** 30b; **Science Museum/Geoff Dann:**
BC; **Science Photo Library:** 11, 36tr.

Additional photography by James Stevenson.

Contents

Journey to the Moon

One giant leap   2

Homeward bound   3

The later
years   46

EYEWITNESS ◉ READERS

READING
3
ALONE

SPACEBUSTERS

THE RACE TO THE MOON

In 1961 the President of the United States made a pledge that America would send a man to the Moon before the end of the 1960s. Here is the story of the final stage of that race against time.

Written by Philip Wilkinson

DORLING KINDERSLEY
London • New York • Sydney

Journey to the Moon

Three, two, one – blast off! With a great roar the Apollo 11 rocket lifted off the ground. Flames and smoke poured from its base as it started its dangerous journey to the Moon.

President Kennedy had promised an American would reach the Moon before the end of the 1960s. It was already the summer of 1969. The astronauts had the chance to make history!

But Commander Neil Armstrong's heart pounded. He and his crew had only a fifty-fifty chance of returning alive.

Take-off, July 16, 1969

The three astronauts were, from left to right, Neil Armstrong, Michael Collins and Edwin Aldrin.

Armstrong kept an eye on the instrument panel. He watched the lights and dials change as the rocket quickly picked up speed.

Soon they were travelling 25,000 miles an hour – thirty times faster than a jet-plane. The force pushed the men back into their seats and made it difficult to move.

The entire spacecraft was taller than a thirty-storey building. Most of this was a rocket that held fuel. When the fuel was used up, the rocket was released. The astronauts continued their journey in a capsule called the Command Module.

Getting rid of the rocket
After nearly 12 minutes the rocket, now empty of fuel, broke away and fell to the ground.

Commander Neil Armstrong

Armstrong turned to talk to Edwin
Aldrin. It would take three days to reach
the Moon, and Armstrong wanted to go
over their planned landing.

Aldrin had spent years studying space. He looked forward to walking on the Moon and doing experiments there.

While Armstrong and Aldrin worked, the third astronaut, Michael Collins, got himself something to eat. Since everything in the spacecraft was weightless, ordinary food would float off a plate. Collins had to eat what looked like baby food from a plastic bag.

All the food had been dried to store it for the journey, so it had to be mixed with water. But there was plenty of choice, including beef and chicken.

Space food

Astronauts added water to dried food to make it sticky. This way no crumbs could float around and damage the spacecraft's controls.

As the spacecraft sped towards the Moon the three men rested. They needed to save their energy so they would be wide awake for the dangers of the Moon landing ahead.

Out in space the Sun's heat is fierce. The capsule turned around and around. This stopped it from getting too hot on one side and burning up.

Sometimes when the men looked out of the windows they could see Earth. It was shining brightly and looked like a beautiful, giant disc in the sky.

Landing craft attached to the Command Module

The astronauts planned to set down on an area of the Moon called the Sea of Tranquility. It was not a real sea because there is no water on the Moon.

From Earth, the Sea of Tranquility looked like a flat plain – a good surface to land on.

On schedule, the spacecraft circled the Moon, sending pictures back to Earth. Then the big moment arrived. It was time for two of the astronauts to try to land.

Armstrong and Aldrin prepared to leave the Command Module and enter the small landing craft that would take them to the Moon. They climbed through the craft's narrow hatch. The craft was nicknamed Eagle but it looked more like a giant metal spider.

Collins stayed in the Command Module and pressed a button. Slowly the two crafts separated. Then the Eagle headed for the Moon's surface with its passengers on board.

As Armstrong and Aldrin drew close, they could see the surface more clearly.

The Moon did not look flat enough to land on. It was peppered with craters and covered in boulders the size of small cars. They could not see a smooth place to set down.

The Eagle came closer and closer to the Moon. It was steered by a computer. But this computer couldn't see the dangerous surface ahead. It kept them straight on course. They were going to crash-land in a huge crater!

Armstrong decided to take over, and he grabbed the controls. Now he was flying the landing craft on his own.

Steering the landing craft

Sixteen small rockets spaced around the landing craft were used to make the craft move right or left, up or down.

"How's the fuel?" he asked Aldrin.

"Eight per cent," Aldrin replied. This meant there was very little landing fuel left. They had only seconds to land!

Mission Control

Scientists directed the flight from Mission Control in Texas. The person who spoke to the astronauts was called the CapCom.

Armstrong spotted a smooth place. Quickly he began to bring the craft straight down. Moon dust flew everywhere. Armstrong could not see where they were going.

Then he heard Aldrin say, "Contact light." They were down! Armstrong pressed the button marked engine stop. Then he radioed Mission Control on Earth. "The Eagle has landed," he announced. ❖

One giant leap

Neil Armstrong wanted to get out and explore the Moon straight away. But he knew it was important to check the spacecraft first. He and Aldrin needed to make it ready for take-off. If they met some unknown danger, they might have to leave the Moon in a hurry.

When the craft was ready, they helped each other put on their outside clothing. They pulled on overshoes. Then they put on helmets with visors to reflect the Sun's blinding light.

Space clothing

A spacesuit is like a miniature spacecraft. It has everything the astronaut needs to survive outside the craft, such as a radio, oxygen and watertight pouches to store urine. The astronauts can even sip drinks inside their suits.

helmet

oxygen
supply
connection

nappy
cover

lunar
glove

lunar
overshoe

detachable
pocket

protective
inner shoe

ARMSTRONG

NASA

ARMSTRONG

21

Each man also wore a huge backpack. It contained an oxygen supply so he could breathe. The packs were heavy, but everything is lighter on the Moon because there is less gravity, so the men could carry them with ease.

"All set for gloves?" Aldrin asked. Once these were on, the spacesuits were complete.

Then each man flicked a switch. Motors in the backpacks began to hum quietly. Aldrin felt a whoosh on his face as oxygen filled his helmet. They were ready to go outside.

The force of gravity
This force holds people on the ground. When people experience gravity weaker than it is on Earth, they feel lighter and can float.

Cameras in the landing craft sent pictures back to Mission Control on Earth. As the scientists watched, Armstrong pushed the hatch open and stepped through the gap.

Armstrong climbed carefully down the nine rungs towards the Moon's surface. He could see that the Moon was covered in a light dust. "It's almost like powder," he said into his radio to Mission Control. He hoped his feet would find firm ground.

Then he stepped off the last rung. Under the dust the ground was hard. Armstrong was elated. He was the first human being ever to stand on the Moon. His next words were heard all over the Earth. "That's one small step for man, one giant leap for mankind."

Landing-craft feet
The landing craft had wide feet to stop it from sinking into the Moon. Gold foil helped protect the feet from the cold.

Neil Armstrong looked over the bleak and barren landscape. Then he raised his camera and took some photographs.

A scoop is used to collect rock

Next he bent over to collect samples for scientists on Earth. He filled a bag with dust, adding some rocks for good measure.

Armstrong was overjoyed. He had collected one bag of Moon samples. Now it was time for some fun. He threw away the handle of the collecting bag. Even with a gentle underarm throw, the handle travelled a long way. The Moon's gravity was too weak to pull it down.

Aldrin stayed in the landing craft. He watched his friend playing on the Moon's surface. "I didn't know you could throw so far," he joked.

Moon rock
This picture shows a slice of rock from the Moon. Some Moon rock is 4.6 billion years old.

Aldrin was itching to join Armstrong.
At last it was his turn. Aldrin climbed
slowly down the landing craft ladder
and stepped onto the Moon.
He looked down. Wherever
he put his boots, he left clear,
sharp footprints.

Together Aldrin and
Armstrong planted the
American flag. It was hard to push the
flag into the Moon's rough surface.
But once it was up the men stood next
to it and felt proud.

Then Aldrin decided to try running.

Footprints
There is no wind or rain
on the Moon, so the
astronauts' footprints
will remain there for ever.

He made huge strides and bounded like a kangaroo. But he felt as though he was running in slow motion.

Aldrin stands next to the American flag which was stiffened with wire because there is no wind on the Moon.

The astronauts were having fun when Mission Control came on the radio. "The President of the United States would like to say a few words to you."

Armstrong and Aldrin stopped short. They were so busy that they had forgotten people were watching them on television all over the world.

President Richard Nixon spoke briefly to the men. "All the people on this Earth are truly one," he said. "One in their pride in what you have done."

The astronauts got busy – there was work to be done! First they set up a machine that was able to detect any movements on the Moon's surface.

Measuring instrument
This showed that it is 390,000 km (240,000 miles) from the Earth to the Moon. That's more than nine times around the world.

The machine would send this information back to Earth. They also set up an instrument to help scientists measure the distance from the Earth to the Moon.

The men worked for two and a half hours, then returned to the Eagle to rest. They had to be alert to take off and dock with the Command Module which was orbiting the Moon. One mistake and they could drift off into space and be lost for ever.

Armstrong and Aldrin climbed into the landing craft and closed the hatch. They were covered in Moon dust. Some scientists had said the dust could catch fire in oxygen. But the astronauts needed oxygen to breathe. They turned on the air supply and waited. The cabin filled with air. But the dust was safe. It did not ignite.

Then the men tried to rest, but they were too keyed up about lift-off. Collins was circling around the Moon. Would they ever see him again?

Landing craft engine
One engine lifted the landing craft off the Moon. It fired for 7 minutes and 45 seconds and took the astronauts into Moon orbit.

When it was finally time to leave the Moon, Aldrin pressed the button marked proceed. The engine fired up. Moon dust and debris sprayed all around them. They were off! ❖

The landing craft leaves its legs behind at take-off

Homeward bound

While Armstrong and Aldrin were exploring, Collins circled the Moon in the Command Module. For half of each orbit he was on the dark side of the Moon – the side always turned away from the Sun. Everything was silent. No radio signals could reach him. Collins was completely out of contact with the rest of the human race. No one had ever been more alone.

Collins was worried that Armstrong and Aldrin would get stuck on the Moon, or that they wouldn't be able to dock with the Command Module. If either happened he would have to leave his two friends to die in space.

The Command Module orbits the Moon

At last, through his window,
Collins spotted the landing craft coming
towards him. He steered the Command
Module carefully so that the two crafts
lined up ready for docking.

The spacecrafts were almost
touching. One false move and they
could miss each other completely.

Seconds seemed like hours. Then a buzzer sounded and a set of latches closed with a clunk. The landing craft had attached to the Command Module.

Armstrong and Aldrin clambered back into the module. At last Collins could relax. They could all return to Earth together.

It would take three days for the astronauts to reach Earth. They caught up on their sleep while the force of Earth's gravity pulled them back home.

At last, they entered the Earth's atmosphere – the layer of air around the planet. Then the outside of the spacecraft began to heat up. It became 25 times hotter than a kitchen oven.

The spacecraft was protected by a heat shield. Through the window the astronauts could see bits of the shield come off and fly past them. They prayed that the shield would hold out.

Heat shield

Metals light enough for a spacecraft could not resist great heat. So the craft was coated with resin that would burn away and keep it cool.

Crack! The astronauts heard the noise of the first small parachutes, called the drogues, opening above them. The drogues set the craft on an even course, so that it would fall steadily down to Earth.

Whoosh! A small vent opened, bringing air into the cabin. This made the air inside the craft the same as it was on the outside.

Then there was another cracking sound. "There go the mains," said Armstrong. He meant the main parachutes. Now they were floating slowly down. Finally, with a loud splash, they landed in the Pacific Ocean.

The pick-up crew found them
floating there several minutes later.
They seemed fine, but what if they had
brought back new germs from the Moon?
Swimmers threw germ-proof rubber suits
to the astronauts and the men put them
on. It was best not to take any chances.

Back on land, the astronauts had to
be kept apart from other people until
they had been thoroughly tested.
The three men had
to spend about two
weeks locked in a
special laboratory.

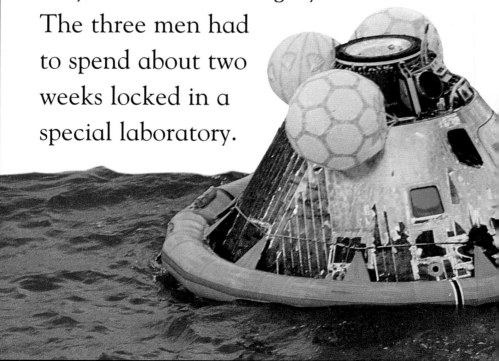

Only their doctors
were supposed to
go in with them.
But some of the
scientists had
touched the Moon

rock samples by accident, and they had
to stay in the lab too.

Then one hot evening the doctors
said the astronauts were all in good
health. The men were allowed out of
the small room at last, free to go home
to their wives and children. ❖

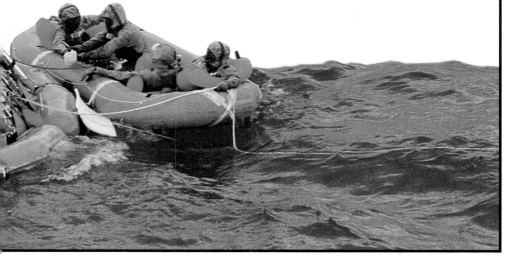

The later years

After Apollo 11 there were five more Apollo missions to the Moon. Some of the astronauts on these missions explored the Moon using a small, battery-powered car called a Lunar Rover.

In 1981 a new spacecraft blasted off – the Space Shuttle. Unlike the Apollo rockets, the Shuttle can fly many missions. Its huge cargo hold carries scientific equipment into space to do work that would be impossible to do on Earth.

Neil Armstrong became a director of the Space Agency in Washington, D.C. He later retired to run a farm in his native Ohio.

Lunar Rover

Shuttle astronauts have been able to repair the Hubble Space Telescope. It provides fascinating images of space.

Astronauts have now lived in orbiting space stations for months at a time. Satellites from Earth have reached the outer limits of our solar system.

The next step? The possibilities are endless – perhaps astronauts on Mars! ❖

Edwin Aldrin became a space engineer, designing spacecraft and planning future missions. He also raises money and support for space research.

Michael Collins became director of the National Air and Space Museum, Washington, D.C. It is said to be the world's most exciting museum.

Glossary

Apollo 11
The spacecraft used to land a human on the Moon for the first time.

Astronauts
Men and women who have been trained to travel in space.

Atmosphere
The layer of air or other gases that surrounds the Earth and other planets.

CapCom
The person at Mission Control who talks directly to the astronauts. CapCom is short for Capsule Communicator.

Command Module
The part of the spacecraft where the astronauts lived and worked during their journey from the Earth to the Moon.

Docking
The joining together of two spacecrafts in space.

Drogues
Three small parachutes that steadied the spacecraft as it fell to Earth.

Gravity
The force that pulls things towards the ground and holds them there.

Heat shield
Protective covering on the outside of the Command Module. The shield kept the craft cool as it neared the Earth.

Laboratory
Room or building where scientific experiments are performed.

Landing craft
The spacecraft that the astronauts used to land on the Moon's surface.

Mission Control
Place in Houston, Texas, U.S.A., where scientists direct the space flight and advise the astronauts.

Orbit
The journey around a planet such as the Earth.

Space
The vast area out from the Earth that contains the planets and stars.

Spacecraft
Any vehicle that is designed for travel in space.

Weightlessness
Lack of weight in space which allows objects to float around.